"PLANET UNDER PRESSURE

Too Many People on Earth?"

Matt Anniss

Gareth Stevens
Publishing

Please visit our website, www.garethstevens.com. For a free color catalog of all our high-quality books, call toll free 1-800-542-2595 or fax 1-877-542-2596.

Library of Congress Cataloging-in-Publication Data

Anniss, Matt.
  Planet under pressure : too many people on earth? / Matt Anniss.
     pages cm. — (Ask an expert)
  Includes index.
  ISBN 978-1-4339-8644-4 (pbk.)
  ISBN 978-1-4339-8645-1 (6-pack)
  ISBN 978-1-4339-8643-7 (library binding)
  1. Overpopulation—Juvenile literature. 2. Nonrenewable natural resources—Juvenile literature I. Title.
  HB883.A56 2013
  363.9—dc23

                              2012037835

First Edition

Published in 2013 by
Gareth Stevens Publishing
111 East 14th Street, Suite 349
New York, NY 10003

Produced by Calcium, www.calciumcreative.co.uk
Designed by Emma DeBanks and Paul Myerscough
Edited by Sarah Eason

Photo credits: Dreamstime: Aedal 44, Antartis 43, Bgupal 39, Djembe 45, Eprom 37, Hungchungchih 36, Jca 22, Sadikgulec 24, 25, Samrat35 34, 35, Urosr 42, Wollwerth 32; Shutterstock: 197lyes 11, ARENA Creative 41, Arindambanerjee 1, 17b, Hector Conesa 23, Robert J. Daveant 15, Sam DCruz 17t, Andy Dean Photography 28, DP Photography 10, Rob van Esch 31, Vladislav Gurfinkel 12, Homeros 9, 16, Frank Jr 40, Kaetana 18, Kataleewan Intarachote 8, Meunierd 4, Mikeledray 26, Monkey Business Images 7, Anton Oparin 29, Chris P. 13, Patrick Poendl 33, Paul Prescott 19, Lev Radin 27, TonyV3112 5, Dana Ward cover, 38, Jaren Jai Wicklund 6, Steshkin Yevgeniy 30, Gary Yim 14.

Printed in the United States of America

CPSIA compliance information: Batch #CW13GS: For further information contact Gareth Stevens, New York, New York at 1-800-542-2595.

Contents

Right now, there are around 7 billion people living on Earth. Sixty years ago, there were just 2.5 billion. In less than the lifespan of the average human, the world's population—the number of people living on the planet—has gone up by an amazing 4.5 billion.

A Ticking Time Bomb?

According to the United Nations, around 134 million babies are born each year. If this continues, in 100 years from now there could be twice the number of people in the world as there are today.

Face Facts

"Humans everywhere must understand that rapid population growth damages the Earth and diminishes human well-being."
David Pimentel, Professor Emeritus at Cornell University

Africa is one of the areas in which the population is rising at incredible rates.

If the world's population keeps growing at current rates, by 2050 there will be 10 billion people on Earth.

Different Viewpoints

Some experts think that there are far too many people on the planet. They say that if the population keeps rising at current rates, we will one day run out of food, clean water, and other resources such as oil, coal, and gas. Other experts disagree. They believe that instead of increasing, in the future the world's population will decrease.

Big Questions

So, should we be worried? Are there too many people living on Earth? If there are, what can we do to change the situation? In this book, we ask the experts for answers to these questions. We'll then ask you to become the expert and make up your own mind about our growing population crisis.

ask the experts

Many experts say that it is not just the world population we need to be concerned about, but the growing populations in our cities. More and more people are moving to cities. We urgently need to build more city housing to cope with the demand of an ever-growing population.

Every year, more and more people are being born around the world. Added to this, in the West, most people are now living for longer than ever before. Our longer lifespans are putting further pressure on resources such as food, oil, and gas. The question is, will Earth be able to provide enough resources for a potentially huge future population?

A Global Crisis

Face Facts

"Think of the Earth as a living organism that is being attacked by billions of bacteria whose numbers double every 40 years. Either the organism dies, the virus dies, or both die."
American writer
Gore Vidal

Parents in the West can expect their children to live longer than them, thanks to advances in healthcare.

Better Health

So why are we living longer? There are two main reasons. The first is the increase in the quality of healthcare. Over the last 100 years, doctors and scientists have found ways to cure many diseases. The invention of vaccines to protect us against disease, and of new methods to treat other illnesses, has cut death rates dramatically.

As more people live long, healthy lives, the number of people on Earth will continue to rise.

More Food

Most people around the world are also healthier because the quality of their diets has improved and they also consume more food. This is because of changes in the way we grow and harvest food crops. The "Green Revolution" of the 1960s and 1970s made food cheaper to produce and buy than ever before for people in the developed world. Because of this, fewer people go hungry and die of starvation than in the past.

"the debate

Experts are divided on the impact of the "Green Revolution" in farming. Some think that in the future it will become too expensive to produce as much food as we do now, and people will starve. Norman Barlaug, the man credited with driving the "Green Revolution," disagrees. He says it has been "a change in the right direction" and "transformed the world."

A Farming Crisis?

As the world's population increases, it puts greater pressure on Earth's natural resources. At present, the world produces more than enough food, and fewer people than ever before go hungry. However, some experts think that if the population keeps increasing, by 2030 there might not be enough food to feed everyone.

Face Facts

"Our food reserves are at a 50-year low, and by 2030 we need to be producing 50 percent more food. If not, many people will starve." Professor John Beddington, Government Chief Scientist for the United Kingdom

Asian farmers currently produce around 500 million tons (454 tonnes) of rice every year, but will they be able to produce more in the future?

People in Africa and Asia may starve if we do not find ways to grow more food.

Running Out of Land

At present, around 12 percent of the land available on Earth is used for growing food. However, experts say there is only an additional 7 to 10 percent of land available to grow more food in the future. If we don't find ways to increase production within the land we already farm, people may starve.

Possible Solutions

Some experts have suggested that the way forward is to build skyscrapers in which food is grown. Others say that people in rich countries should eat and waste less food. At present, Americans throw out more than 200,000 tons (181,000 tonnes) of edible food every day. Many say that we should distribute the food more fairly around the world.

" the debate

Some experts deny that there is a food crisis. In 2000, population experts Michael Haynes and Rumy Hussan wrote: "In a world that now produces more food than is necessary to feed all its population, there is no excuse for hunger." However, many others disagree. They point out that we already use 90 percent of the land that can be farmed, and demand for food will soon be too great for many farmers to cope. "

9

Demand for oil is growing in countries such as India, where the population is rising.

A Fuel Crisis

Demand for natural fuels such as oil, gas, and coal has risen sharply in recent years. This is because of the increasing numbers of people living on Earth. Fuel is needed to power the farming equipment and factories that produce our food. It is also needed to provide power for airplanes and cars, generate electricity, and heat homes. As the world's population increases, people are using up Earth's natural fuels quicker than ever before. We are simply using too much, too quickly for Earth to cope.

Oil Issues

Gas, coal, and oil cannot be made by people. They come from "reserves" deep underground. We already use many of these reserves, and one day, they will run out. Unless we figure out other ways to farm food, generate electricity, and power transportation, we will face an enormous future energy crisis.

Face Facts

"We have enough oil for the next few years. After that, the situation deteriorates."
Chris Skrebowski, Editor, *Petroleum Review*

IS TIME RUNNING OUT?

Exactly how much oil is left in the ground is a matter of great debate. A report by the oil industry in 2007 predicted that there is enough to last another 40 years, but only if the amount we use each year does not increase. As the world's population grows, it is likely we will use more and Earth's oil wells will have run dry before 2050.

Experts agree that we must find alternatives to our current energy supplies.

A Planet in Crisis

Experts claim that we are damaging Earth almost beyond repair. To house and feed everyone, we have cut down forests to build more cities, plundered the planet's natural resources, and built factories that spew toxic gases into the air. As a result, we are running out of usable land, many species of animals and plants have died out, and stocks of natural materials that are needed for building are dwindling very quickly.

Global Warming

Some scientists also believe that the number of humans on Earth, coupled with our reliance on oil as a fuel, is making the world's weather more extreme. This is known as "global warming." Experts say that certain areas of the world are drying out, making it difficult for crops to grow, while storms and floods are drenching other areas.

Experts fear that our effect on the planet is now causing natural disasters such as hurricanes.

Face Facts

"The human impact on the planet could be the loss of all species by the end of the twenty-first century." Peter Raven, former President of the American Association for the Advancement of Science

Experts say that global warming caused by our reliance on oil is melting the ice at the top and bottom of the planet.

FRAGILE WORLD

Scientists point out that for the planet to remain a healthy place for humans to live, we need to protect wildlife. We need plants and trees to supply us with oxygen to breathe. By forcing species into extinction, we will disrupt the natural balance of life on our plant. Some scientists believe we have already exceeded the "carrying capacity" of Earth—the number of people the planet can sustain without being damaged beyond repair forever.

" the debate

Not all scientists agree that humans are to blame for global warming. Some say it is part of a natural increase in the planet's temperature over many millions of years.

"

In Brazil, many people live together in poorly-built shacks in areas called "favelas."

ask the experts

The United Nations believes that building bigger cities may be the best way to cope with population growth. This is because cities concentrate people in a relatively small area, which minimizes damage to the natural world. By building better cities with better facilities, we could save lives and the world we live in.

A Housing Crisis

Two of the most pressing problems linked to overpopulation are poverty and overcrowding. If someone is living in poverty, it means they are so poor they do not have enough money to buy food or proper shelter. In many places around the world, a large part of the population lives in poverty. They are forced to live on the streets, or crowd into tiny, run-down homes. These homes are often made of whatever can be found, from pieces of concrete and wood to sections of plastic and sheets of corrugated iron.

Shantytowns

Overcrowding is a problem in many cities around the world. In certain parts of Asia, Africa, and South America, poor people are forced to live in "shantytowns." These are large areas full of poorly constructed and crowded housing, barely fit for people to live in. Disease is widespread. According to recent figures, more than 1 billion people around the world live in shantytowns.

SHIFTING THE PROBLEM

Some people in developing countries are prepared to move to richer countries in the hope of finding a better life. This in turn leads to more overcrowded cities, more disease, and more problems. These problems will just get worse as the world's population increases in size over the years.

ONE PROBLEM REPLACES ANOTHER

The dream of a better life in a new country is not always fulfilled. Many of the people who have traveled from developing countries to developed countries have found themselves living in poor conditions. Sometimes, their new lives are hardly better than those they left behind.

Many people move to the United States each year in search of a better life.

Face Facts

"An ever-growing demand for resources by a growing population is threatening our future security, health, and well-being."
Jim Leape,
International Director,
World Wildlife Fund

While population numbers have been increasing all over the world, the most dramatic rises have been seen in what we call the "third world," traditionally poor countries in places such as Africa, Asia, and some parts of South America.

A Developing Crisis

In some African countries, the population has increased by 40 or 50 percent in less than 10 years. The African state of Chad had a population of just over 6 million in 1993. In 2009, it topped 10 million for the first time.

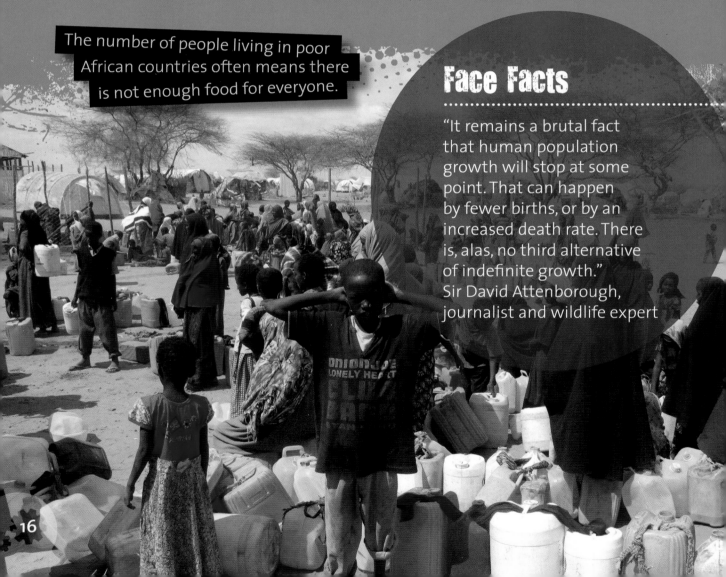

The number of people living in poor African countries often means there is not enough food for everyone.

Face Facts

"It remains a brutal fact that human population growth will stop at some point. That can happen by fewer births, or by an increased death rate. There is, alas, no third alternative of indefinite growth."
Sir David Attenborough, journalist and wildlife expert

Unhealthy living conditions contribute to the problems created by Africa's rapid population growth.

HEALTHCARE MIRACLE

So why has the population rise been greatest in the third world? As in other parts of the world, greater access to healthcare there has meant that many people are living longer. This, coupled with a massive increase in the number of children being born, has led to the population of some countries spiraling out of control.

Children in Africa face severe health and social problems as a result of overcrowding.

MASS POVERTY

Many third world countries do not have the money or the facilities to cope with rapid population growth. Most people are very poor, and there is often not enough housing, food, and clean water for everyone. Because of this, disease and death are rife. Yet, even when large numbers of people die, the population just keeps on growing unchecked.

ask the experts

Experts say that one of the main reasons why so many children are being born in third world countries is a lack of knowledge about what we call "birth control." Opposition to birth control from some religious leaders also plays a big part.

India in Crisis

Nowhere in the world is population growth more out of control than in India. In 1951, just four years after the country gained independence from British rule, the population stood at a sizeable 361.7 million.

Sixty years later, in 2011, that had grown to 1.2 billion, an increase of 245 percent. There are now simply too many people in the country to feed, water, clothe, and shelter. If India's population keeps growing at its current rate, 1.7 billion people will live there by 2030. This will be the largest population of any country on Earth. Will the country be able to cope with this enormous population?

Face Facts

"Humans are 10,000 times more common than we should be."
Steve Jones, Head of the Department of Biology at University College London, United Kingdom

Millions of Indians live on the streets. The luckier ones live in tents and shanty-style huts.

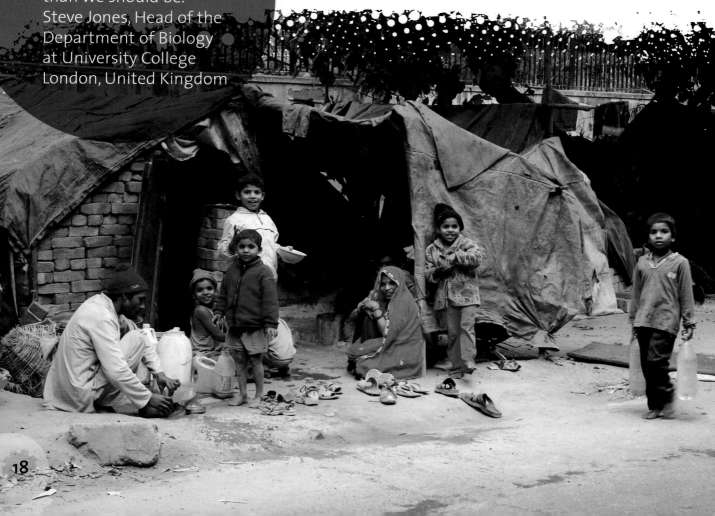

MASS POPULATION, MASS MISERY

Overcrowding in India has already resulted in huge areas of slum housing in its cities, mass starvation, and a high rate of death in babies and children. There is also mass unemployment, no education for millions of children, and no healthcare for the majority of people who live in the country. Overpopulation means misery for millions of Indians.

THE FUTURE FOR INDIA

Unless population growth is controlled in India, the outlook is bleak. Some other countries have started taking steps to cut birth rates. Will India now have to follow suit, too?

Too many babies means too many people. Around 70,000 babies are born In India each day.

ask the experts

Population experts agree that the only way to control the population growth is to limit birth rates in areas such as India, where it is out of control. We will look at how this may be done, and what happened when China tried this method of population control, later in this book.

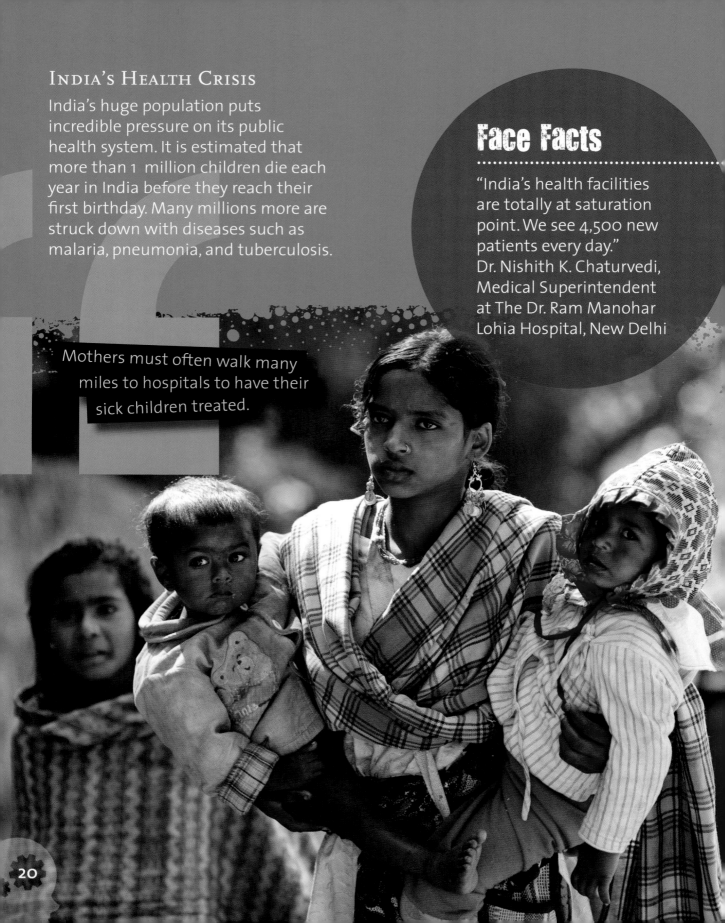

India's Health Crisis

India's huge population puts incredible pressure on its public health system. It is estimated that more than 1 million children die each year in India before they reach their first birthday. Many millions more are struck down with diseases such as malaria, pneumonia, and tuberculosis.

Face Facts

"India's health facilities are totally at saturation point. We see 4,500 new patients every day."
Dr. Nishith K. Chaturvedi, Medical Superintendent at The Dr. Ram Manohar Lohia Hospital, New Delhi

Mothers must often walk many miles to hospitals to have their sick children treated.

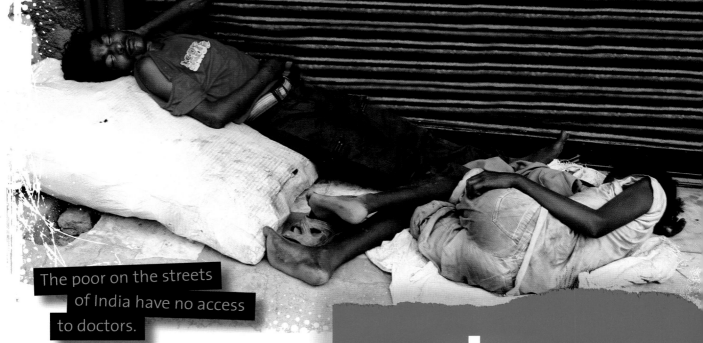

The poor on the streets of India have no access to doctors.

FAR TOO LITTLE, TOO LATE

Sickness and disease are major problems in India, because so many people live in poverty and have little access to medical treatment. Death rates from curable diseases are worst in remote, rural areas. To get treatment, people are often forced to travel for many miles to find a hospital. India's health system is stretched to the breaking point.

FIGHTING BACK

India has shown that it is capable of fighting back against disease and poverty. In 2012, India's prime minister announced that in the past year not a single new case of polio had been recorded. Polio is a deadly disease that had already been wiped out in most of the world. India is now polio-free for the first time in history.

ask the experts

Health experts agree that millions of children will keep dying in India every year unless the government commits billions more dollars to fighting malnutrition, tuberculosis, and malaria. As many of these diseases have simply built up a resistance to the drugs currently used to fight them, it will mean developing new vaccines, fast.

GIANT EFFORT

India's success in eradicating polio is due to a huge effort from the government, medical services, and global charities. More than $1 billion has been spent on making and delivering polio vaccines. Doctors and charity workers were sent to the most remote parts of the country to give vaccine injections to children. The process took a huge amount of time and effort, but it has been a great success.

Millions of Africans suffer from HIV/AIDS, yet have very little healthcare to support them.

AFRICA IN CRISIS

Despite all of India's problems, its economy is developing rapidly and the government has money to spend on healthcare programs. The same cannot be said for many countries in Africa, where population growth, overcrowding, and poverty are almost as bad. There, many Africans face a daily struggle for survival. Many women give birth to a high number of children during their lives, but living conditions are so bad in some places that several of these children may die before they even reach just five years of age.

RISING BIRTH RATES

Although more people are born in India and China every year than anywhere else on Earth, birth rates are actually far higher in central, west, and northern African countries. This is because birth rate figures are calculated on the number of births per 1,000 people, rather than just the number of people born. This means that, in Africa, more babies are being born to fewer women.

OUT OF CONTROL

The population growth in Africa over the last 60 years has been simply staggering. In 1950, the continent was home to around 230 million people. In 2010, that number stood at more than 1 billion. The rate shows no signs of slowing down, either. In the 10 years between 2000 and 2010, the continent's population grew by more than 25 percent.

Birth rates in many African countries are much higher than in India or China.

ask the experts

Most experts agree that the root of Africa's population problems is poverty. Unless the standard of living of poor Africans is increased, and more people are educated, birth rates will continue to rise and Africa will face an enormous future crisis.

FAMINE IN AFRICA

Many experts worry about the problems of overpopulation in Africa, because of the continent's unique natural difficulties. The continent is one of the hottest places on Earth. This means that much of the soil is dry, full of rocks, and hard to grow crops in. Clean freshwater is also scarce. Droughts cause local rivers, water holes, and lakes to dry up.

These harsh conditions mean that famines, where hundreds of thousands of people go hungry, are common.

Face Facts

"The economic situation has brought it home to our people that if they want their children to be educated and well fed, then they have to begin to do something about the amount of children they have."
Olikoye Ransome-Kuti, former Minister of Health, Nigeria

When famine strikes Africa, many children go hungry unless rich countries offer food, money, and help.

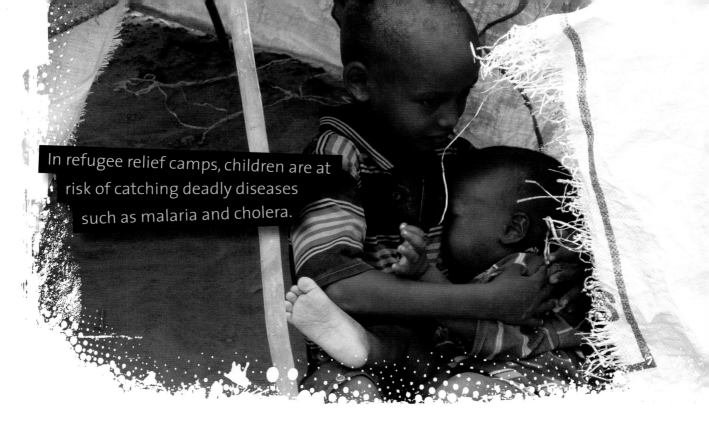

In refugee relief camps, children are at risk of catching deadly diseases such as malaria and cholera.

MAJOR CRISIS

When famine or drought hits an African country, the results can be devastating. The international community does what it can to help, offering money, food, and water. But the stark truth is that there are far too many people starving or dying of dehydration for charities and aid agencies to help. The reality is that little can be done to avoid the deaths of thousands.

DEATH AND DISEASE

When famine strikes an African country, many people travel for hundreds of miles to find relief. When they reach their destination, there is usually nowhere for them to sleep. Charities try to help by setting up huge refugee relief camps. However, the conditions in these camps are often terrible. It is not uncommon for people to die in the camps from diseases picked up by living in dirty conditions, close to sick people.

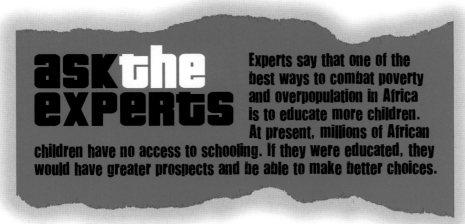

ask the experts

Experts say that one of the best ways to combat poverty and overpopulation in Africa is to educate more children. At present, millions of African children have no access to schooling. If they were educated, they would have greater prospects and be able to make better choices.

It is easy to look at the problems population growth causes in the third world and think it is not our problem. Yet experts say overpopulation is a very real issue for almost every country on Earth, even in rich, developed nations such as the United States and the United Kingdom. Population growth is not just a third world problem—it is a first world problem, too.

A First World Problem

In the West, immigration, a growing population, and a shrinking job market mean that even low-skill jobs are now in demand.

Face Facts

"A doubling in population will plunge us into an age of extinction and desolation unseen since the dinosaurs disappeared 65 million years ago." Chris Hedges, journalist and author

The West is now feeling the impact of a growing population, with fewer jobs and greater poverty.

"the debate"

Some experts believe that population growth is linked to the easy availability of food. They say that when food is cheap and plentiful, the population rises. Other experts do not agree. They point out that the population is growing fastest in poorer countries, where there is less food. Also, the population of rich European countries such as Germany is expected to fall in the next 30 years.

BLAME GAME

Some experts argue that the world's population crisis is not the fault of people in Africa or Asia, but of the developed world. Some scientists in these richer nations have driven advances in healthcare and the mass production of food. It is the people in these wealthier nations, too, who consume most of the world's precious natural resources.

CRITICAL MASS

Birth rates are actually falling in the first world, but that has not stopped population growth because we live longer. For example, the population of North America (the USA and Canada combined) has increased by 25 percent since 1950. In Europe, it has increased by 10 percent. In the West, we are as much to blame for the world's rapidly growing population as developing countries.

In the future, jobs, food, and money in the United States could be in short supply and many people may lose their homes.

THE UNITED STATES IN CRISIS

The United States is a big country, more than big enough to cope with a population that has increased from 76 million in 1901 to 313 million in 2012. Yet some experts say that the country is already overcrowded. According to population expert David Pimentel of Cornell University, the United States can only cope with a population of 200 million. He says that if the US population is not reduced by at least one-third, in the future there will not be enough food, jobs, or money for every citizen within the country.

RISING AND FALLING

The United Nations does not believe that US population growth will slow down in the near future. According to government projections, the country's population will grow by nearly 50 percent in the next 40 years. Yet birth rates in the United States have been falling for the last 30 years, and are predicted to continue to fall over the next few years.

The Immigrant's Tale

The reason for the projected increase in the number of people living in the United States is simple—immigration. The country has always welcomed people from other countries, and many Americans can trace their roots back to Europe, Africa, and South America. This trend looks likely to increase, meaning many more problems for the future.

As the US population continues to grow, more people may be forced to live on the streets.

ask the experts

Experts agree that if the United States does not bring its population growth under control soon, the country will begin to run out of food. The gap between the richest and poorest will increase, and social unrest may follow. The country one day may even be forced to go to war to secure vital fuel and food supplies for its millions of people.

Homeless Alone, Hungry & Cold! All Acts of Kindness greatly Appreciated Thank You. Cheers

MORE THAN OUR FAIR SHARE

The United States uses almost twice as many resources as it produces. Americans own 30 percent of all the cars in the world, pump more toxic gases into Earth's atmosphere, and use up more than 20 percent of the oil produced in the world each year. What's more, the average American uses 105 gallons (400 liters) of water every day, compared to the 2 gallons (10 liters) used by people in the world's developing countries.

NO WAY BACK

Population experts say these statitistics are unsustainable. This means that people in developed countries such as the United States cannot continue to use up the world's resources this quickly. We are taking more than our fair share, and it's time to reconsider.

Due to overconsumption, the average American produces 75 tons (68 tonnes) of trash by the time they are 75 years old.

Face Facts

"Infinite growth of consumption in a finite world is an impossibility." E. F. Schumacher, economist and writer

Our Western obsession with the latest goods is driving us to overconsumption and eventual self-destruction.

Overconsumption

Excessive consumption of natural resources is called overconsumption. Experts believe that as the world's population continues to grow, the problem of overconsumption in rich nations will reach crisis levels. More people on Earth means more demand for food, fuel, and water. Unless the West can cut down its consumption of resources, more people will die in Africa, Asia, and poor parts of South America. Eventually, the West will starve, too.

ask the experts

Most experts agree that the only solution to overconsumption in developed countries is to slow the rate at which we are using up resources such as oil and natural gas. However, this would require new laws from governments. These would be very unpopular with most people, and it is very unlikely we will see them in the near future.

UNPOPULAR SOLUTIONS

Governments around the world realize that rich countries must reduce their consumption of natural resources in response to the growing population crisis. Some experts think that the only way to slow down population growth is to lift poor countries out of poverty. That means allowing them to use more resources, while richer countries in the West must use fewer.

IMPORTANT AGREEMENT

Since the late 1990s, many governments around the world have been trying to reach an agreement to reduce the amount of energy they use. In 2005, an agreement was reached in Japan in which most of the world's governments agreed to cut down their energy use. Only one major nation would not sign the Kyoto Protocol—the United States.

Face Facts

"Each American puts out about 20 tons (18 tonnes) of carbon dioxide gases every year. Somehow, we have to make changes that will bring that down to zero." Bill Gates, founder, Microsoft

Big Failure

The idea behind the Kyoto Protocol was that developed countries would limit the amount of harmful gases they released into the air through their oil refineries and other factories. To do so, developed countries would use less oil and save precious oil resources for future use. It would also mean that fewer harmful gases would be released into the atmosphere, to counter those released by developing countries as their industries increase.

ask the experts

Many experts have questioned the success of the Kyoto Protocol. They say that because the US government did not sign up, it will be doomed to failure. Unless the United States radically reduces its consumption of energy, other countries may back out of the agreement, and we'll be no further forward.

Using wind to generate electricity rather than oil, gas, or coal could be one answer to our energy problems.

The world's growing population is like a ticking bomb. For every year that we continue to do nothing to stop it, we get nearer to catastrophe.

Radical Solutions

Population experts say that the time for simple action has passed. We need to think about more radical solutions to solve Earth's population crisis.

Face Facts

"Those who oppose birth control are either incapable of arithmetic or in favor of war and famine as permanent features of human life." Bertrand Russell, philosopher

Experts say that reducing the number of babies people have is the key to tackling population growth.

Two Key Aims

Experts agree that there are two things that need to be done to avert disaster and slow down the population explosion. The first, as we have seen, is to share the world's resources more fairly. That means persuading people in wealthy nations to reduce the resources that they use. The second is somehow to control the growing number of people who are being born around the world.

A Difficult Problem

Slowing the birth rate is not easy. One way to do it is to make everyone richer, as statistics show that birth rates are falling rapidly in the world's wealthiest countries. However, this method would take many, many years, possibly even a century. Other methods that would get quicker results include better education about family planning and laws to limit the number of children people can have.

Governments may have to take drastic action to stop people from having a lot of children.

ask the experts

Population experts have been advising for years that we slow down birth rates around the world. The question is, are our governments listening? Most governments are uncomfortable with spending more money on birth control, or introducing laws that prevent people from making a choice about the number of children that they have.

CHINA'S SOLUTION

China is the most highly populated country on the planet, with well over 1.3 billion people. That figure would be even higher if the country's communist government had not introduced its highly controversial population control policies in 1979. Since then, Chinese couples living in towns and cities in the country have been banned from having more than just one child.

DRASTIC MEASURES

China's "one child policy" was introduced after the country's population almost doubled in the 30 years between 1949 and 1979. The government was worried about the effects of overpopulation in cities, so decided to allow married couples to have only one child. Today, the policy remains in place. The government says it has prevented 200–300 million births, but many doubt this is true.

" the debate

So has the one child policy been a success? The Chinese government claims that it has reduced problems associated with overpopulation, and helped the nation become far richer. However, critics doubt the link between the country's wealth and population control. They say that wealth is only partially responsible for the drop in birth rates. "

China decided to introduce population control measures to combat their overpopulation problems.

Is China's one child policy a solution to overpopulation, or is it a problem instead?

SUCCESS OR FAILURE?

Since China's one child policy was introduced, birth rates have fallen significantly. However, critics point out that as China's population is still growing fast, the policy has not been a success. They say it has also led to more secret births, and the brutal treatment of couples that break the ban. It has also caused other problems, such as a shortage of children to care for their parents when they become old.

Face Facts

"China's population is aging fast. The first children born under the one child policy face the prospect of caring for an ever-increasing number of old people. The clock is ticking."
Weiliang Nie,
BBC China Service

THE BIRTH CONTROL ISSUE

Few countries are willing to follow China's example by forcibly limiting the number of children people have. Many, however, are looking more closely at the issues of birth control and family planning. Already, many Western countries encourage couples to think about how many children to have, and when. Now countries such as India are also encouraging their citizens to do the same.

Face Facts

"We are given two choices to deal with overpopulation—famine, pestilence, and war on one hand, birth control on the other. Most of us choose birth control."
Aldous Huxley, writer

The use of contraceptives could be a solution to India's growing population crisis.

The Indian government recently pledged nearly $1 billion to provide people with free birth control aids.

FAMILY PLANNING

Birth control is the process of reducing the number of births by encouraging people to use contraception. Using contraception stops a woman from becoming pregnant. In some countries, contraceptives are given out free of charge to reduce the number of unwanted pregnancies.

CHURCH OBJECTIONS

Although contraceptives are widely used around the world, they are frowned upon by some religions. United Nations officers reported hearing Muslim leaders in Africa telling people not to use contraceptives, while the Catholic Church is also strongly opposed to contraception.

ask the experts

Population experts agree that birth control is the quickest way to slow down population growth around the world. They say that it is vital to educate people in developing nations about family planning and contraceptives. This way, they might choose to have fewer children. This is something that many people in developed countries in the West are already doing.

The Politics of Population

Over recent years, many population experts, scientists, and writers have called on governments worldwide to act now to stop Earth's population from spiraling out of control. Yet governments have mostly done very little. So why are they not listening to expert warnings?

Controversial Ideas

Many of the solutions proposed to slow down population growth are controversial. They mostly require passing laws to limit our use of natural resources, or the number of children we can have. While these sorts of laws may be needed to avert a crisis in 50 or 100 years' time, most politicians only think in the short term. They are concerned about getting re-elected at the next election. Introducing these measures would be unpopular, and no politician will risk policies that could lose votes.

The US government has so far not introduced laws to tackle population growth in the United States.

Face Facts

"The chief cause for the impending collapse of the world is the enormous growth of the human population. The worst enemy of life is too much life."
Pentti Linkola, ecologist and writer

No Action in the United States

In the United States, where swift action is probably needed, there is little likelihood of politicians passing new birth control or energy-saving laws in the near future. This is because they would be seen as limiting basic human freedoms, such as the right to choose how many children you have. Any proposed laws would also face opposition from religious groups.

Is it time for the government to limit the number of children in American families?

ask the experts

Most population experts believe that the time for government action on population is now. They say that a failure to introduce laws and policies to slow population growth would doom human life to almost certain extinction. However, few believe governments will actually take any action, despite the expert evidence that backs up their claims.

ROOM FOR MORE?

For all the doom, gloom, and warnings of harsh times ahead, not all experts agree that overpopulation is a problem. Some even argue that Earth can cope with far more people without being damaged beyond repair. Is this really the case? According to a United Nations report in 2003, the world population will peak in 2050. After that, it will stay at the same level until 2300. Other experts predict that after 2050, the world's population will start falling as a natural response to overpopulation.

A few experts say there is no problem with overpopulation, in Africa or elsewhere.

Face Facts

"The population explosion is an uncontrolled multiplication of the human race. The disease is so far advanced that only with radical surgery does the patient have a chance to survive." Paul R. Eidrich, US biologist and author

Some scientists have proposed leaving Earth altogether, to set up homes elsewhere on other planets.

CONTROVERSIAL IDEAS

Other experts disagree strongly with this opinion. They have urged the world to look for more radical solutions. One such solution is sterilization—the process of making people infertile, so they are incapable of producing offspring. Some highly controversial scientists have suggested a system of sterilization in which people have just one or two children. It is a radical proposal and has little support.

SPACE SOLUTION

In the 1970s, a small group of scientists in the United States came up with another extreme solution to the problem—setting up new homes on other planets. In 1999, a scientist named

Gerard Freeman proposed setting up "human colonies" in deep space. He believes this could happen within centuries, although very few other scientists currently agree with him.

ask the experts

Population expert Dr. Alex Berzow does not believe that overpopulation is a major issue. He says that as countries such as India and China develop and begin to get richer, their people will enjoy the benefits of this new wealth, and population rises will naturally begin to slow.

So, which side are you on? Is the rapid growth of the human population putting the very survival of Earth at risk, or are scientists worrying about nothing? Do we need to think of radical solutions to a growing crisis, or can we just let nature take its course?

You're the Expert

Do you think it is right to control immigration for the sake of population control in the United States?

IMMIGRATION OFFICERS VIOLATE MY HUMAN RIGHTS

Face Facts

"The truth is that the population bomb is being defused around the world. But the consumption bomb is still primed and ever more dangerous." Fred Pearce, author, *Peoplequake*

Running Out of Time?

The arguments for action on population growth are very strong. For thousands of years, the human population of Earth could be counted in millions, rather than billions. There are now 6 billion more humans on Earth than there were 100 years ago. The planet has only a limited amount of natural resources. Do you think the human race can continue to use up Earth's resources and still be around in a few thousands years' time?

Can we solve mass poverty in developing countries by reducing consumption in the West?

"the debate

One of the most vocal opponents of the idea of overpopulation is a group called the Population Research Institute (PRI). They say that overpopulation is a myth, created by some scientists to push through their personal beliefs. Scientists have hit back, pointing out that the PRI is funded not by scientific institutions, but by religious organizations that are against birth control.

Nothing to Worry About?

On the other side of the debate, scientists point out that the human race has overcome a lot of obstacles in the last 2,000 years. We are inventive and adaptable, and will find new ways to grow food and produce more energy, such as harnessing the power of the sun, water, or wind. Do you think we will find answers to our population growth and find ways to live sustainably? If you were the expert, what would you decide?

Glossary

birth control measures used to limit the number of children people have

brutal severe

calculated figured out

charities organizations set up to raise money in order to help people who are poor or sick

consumption using goods or services, such as food, fuel, or water

contraception the process of stopping women from having children by use of contraceptives (see below)

contraceptives medicines or other methods used to prevent women from getting pregnant

drought a long period of low rainfall that results in the drying up of natural water resources such as rivers and lakes

edible safe to eat

educated sent to school to learn to read and write

election the process of selecting a government, where people vote for their preferred politicians

eradicating destroying or getting rid of something, for example a deadly disease

exceeded gone past an agreed limit

extinction when the last of a species of animal or plant dies out

family planning the process of deciding when to have children, and how many

famine what happens when a country cannot produce enough food to feed its population, usually because of severe heat or other extreme weather conditions

finite limited

global warming rising world temperatures that may be causing extreme weather events

life expectancy how long someone is expected to live

malnutrition a condition in which a person does not have enough food to maintain good health

overpopulation when there are too many people in a certain place and not enough money, food, water, or homes for everyone

plundered taken a lot of something

politician a person who is chosen by the people of a country to make decisions and to represent them in government

population the number of people living in a certain place

population control measures taken to limit the number of people in a certain country or region, such as limiting the number of children that people can have

poverty not having enough money to live to an acceptable standard

projections forecasts or predictions of what may happen in the future, based on known facts

radical extreme

refugee relief camps temporary camps set up to provide food, water, and shelter for people who have lost their homes because of war, famine, or drought

third world a term used to describe poorer, less developed countries, usually in places such as Africa and Asia

United Nations a worldwide organization featuring representatives from all countries, designed to discuss and deal with global issues

vaccines medicines given to people to stop them from catching certain diseases

Books

Ash, Russell. *The World in One Day.* London, United Kingdom: Dorling Kindersley, 1997.

Barber, Nicola. *The Environment Challenge: Coping with Population Growth.* Chicago, IL: Raintree, 2012.

Menzel, P., and Charles C. Mann. *Material World: A Global Family Portrait.* San Francisco, CA: Sierra Club Books, 1994.

For More Information

Websites

How many people are there currently on Earth? Find out at:
www.census.gov/main/www/popclock.html

National Geographic has a special website looking at the issue of population. Are there too many people on Earth? Find out at:
http://ngm.nationalgeographic.com/7-billion

A short film explaining how the world's population has grown in the last 2,000 years can be found at:
www.youtube.com/watch?v=4BbkQiQyaYc

Publisher's note to educators and parents: Our editors have carefully reviewed these websites to ensure that they are suitable for students. Many websites change frequently, however, and we cannot guarantee that a site's future contents will continue to meet our high standards of quality and educational value. Be advised that students should be closely supervised whenever they access the Internet.

Index